MW01201657

This Belongs To

Made in the USA
Middletown, DE
12 August 2024

58998406R00057